I Promise You My Love

A collection of poems on love
Edited by Susan Polis Schutz

Blue Mountain Press ™

Boulder, Colorado

Copyright © Stephen Schutz and Susan Polis Schutz, 1981.

All rights reserved, including the right to reproduce this book or
portions thereof in any form.

Library of Congress Number: 80-70427
ISBN: 0-88396-129-6

Manufactured in the United States of America
First Printing: February, 1981

The following works have previously appeared in Blue Mountain Arts
publications:

"When we met," "Words are so inadequate," and "In order to
have," by Susan Polis Schutz. "There is nothing more wonderful," by J.
Russell Morrison. "You are the person," by Rebecca J. Barrett.
Copyright © Continental Publications, 1979. All rights reserved.
"Sometimes I get lonely," and "Sometimes when we ," by Laine
Parsons. "For all you have done," "We have something special," and
"With time enough for love . . .," by Andrew Tawney. "I feel more
love" and "Love Is," by Jamie Delere. Copyright © Blue Mountain
Arts, Inc., 1980. All rights reserved.

Thanks to the Blue Mountain Arts creative staff, with special thanks to
Jody Cone, Faith Hamilton, Douglas Pagels and Patti Wayant.

ACKNOWLEDGMENTS are on page 64

Blue Mountain Press INC.

P.O. Box 4549, Boulder, Colorado 80306

CONTENTS

I promise you
my love,
For today
and tomorrow;
I promise you
as much happiness
as I can give;
I promise not
to doubt
or mistrust you,
But to grow
and add to your life
of content.
I promise
never to try to
change you,
But will accept
the changes you make
in yourself;
And I will accept
your love for me
without fear
of tomorrow;
knowing that
tomorrow,
I'll love you more
than I do today.

—Donna Pawluk

I want to love you
   and always be with you
Share all life's pleasures
   and heartaches with you . . .
Make every plan and
   dream each dream with you
And I want to help you
   comfort and love you
I want to always be with you

—Dolly Parton

Sometimes I get lonely
    and thinking about you helps
reminding me that there is
    a person
I cherish so very much
    always close in spirit
    even when you're
    so far away

But sometimes it hurts even more
    to think of you . . .
    your laugh, your touch
    and to remember just
How much I miss
    your gentle face
    your tender ways
    your presence in my life

                    —Laine Parsons

When we met
I was overwhelmed with the
idea of
you
When we got to know each other
I learned that you were a person
with strengths and weaknesses
like everyone else
When we got closer
I was overwhelmed with the
idea of
love
Now as time has passed
I am no longer overwhelmed
with the idea of you and love
but I am more than overwhelmed
with you and the love we share

—Susan Polis Schutz

...You know that
nothing can ever
change what we
have always been
and always will be
to each other.

—Franklin D. Roosevelt

You are the person I am
always thinking of
You are the most important
person in the whole
world to me

You are the one I love

—Rebecca J. Barrett

Thank you for your
presence in my life . . .
you encourage me to go
beyond myself.

—Linda DuPuy Moore

Is it possible to
love someone too much . . .
if it is, that's how I love you.
I guess by that I'm saying,
I love you and it hurts . . .
You're miles away,
and when I'm lonely
and you are all that's
on my mind, it hurts . . . a lot
But then when I pick myself back up,
I realize . . . you're worth it,
and loving too much . . .
is just enough.

—Kathy Ward

I fell in love
with what I expected
you to be—

I love
what I've discovered
    you are.

—Dale F. Mead

You . . .
are something to me
between dream and miracle.

—Elizabeth Barrett Browning

There is nothing more
    wonderful in the world
than the feeling
    you get from sharing,
and there is no
    greater happiness
than the warmth
    you get from loving.

—J. Russell Morrison

Sometimes when we
simply say, "I love you"
we forget that it's not
  a simple thing at all
  or a saying we can lightly use

May we always remember
where we've come from
to reach our
"I love you's"
and where we're going
to whisper more

—Laine Parsons

With time enough for love . . .

When there's time enough for love—
the world's a finer place
where visions are never ending
and serenity is ever beginning . . .
with time enough for love.

When there's time enough for love—
the morning finds the two of us
warming from within
never wanting to be without,
and our days are spent more wisely now . . .
with time enough for love.

When there's time enough for love—
the little things can mean a lot
a longing look, a playful glance,
a quiet time, a tender touch . . .
making "big" problems lose their significance
and reminding us
what a real pleasure the day can bring . . .
   with time enough for love.

When there's time enough for love—
the words we say are special ones
giving and forgiving, soothing,
smoothing the troubled times,
celebrating the joyous ones,
making us aware of the beauty
life has blessed us with . . .

with time enough for love,
and love to last through time.

—Andrew Tawney

I feel more love
    for you
than I imagined
    could be felt in a lifetime

I find more happiness
    in you
than I thought
    I could find

    in all the world.

                —Jamie Delere

When you want to do something
   to make me happy
You need only think of what
   would make yourself happy
Because
   you are a reflection of me
   and I am a reflection of you
When two people are so in love
and share such implicit trust
   as we do
There can only be lasting happiness

—Ken Lewis

When I was young, I dreamed
of finding someone really special
who would come into my life
and love me wholly and uniquely . . .
someone who would understand my desires,
encourage my efforts,
and share my dreams . . .

When I grew older
I found that person:

I love you
for loving me
just the way
I dreamed it would be.

—Linda DuPuy Moore

Because of your love,
I have grown into a new person.
I have experienced new feelings;
I have learned what it is to
    give and accept freely.
You have shown me how to grow
    for myself, in my own way.
In doing so, I have grown
    toward you
        with you
            and for you.
Because of my love,
I hope that you have too.

—Jenny Deeter

I cannot promise you
    a lifetime
        or even a day
For my days and yours
    are bound to others
        through a lifetime commitment...

What I can offer
  is simply
    Me
For whatever amount of time
  we can steal
I offer you laughter
  for laughter is beauty
I offer you honesty
  for honesty is pure
I offer you patience
  for patience is needed to gain trust
I offer you sincerity
  for through my sincerity I will show
  you my inner being and desires . . .
All I ask in return
  is for you to be honest and open
  for through your honesty and
    openness
I will receive from you
  all that I offer

—Roger C. Van Horn

Our love is strengthened
by knowing that
each of us could survive
on our own
    if we wanted to . . .
but realizing that
    more than anything . . .
we choose to be together.

—Sue Mitchell

To renounce your individuality,
   to see with another's eyes,
   to hear with another's ears
To be two and yet one,
   to so melt and mingle
   that you no longer know
   you are you or another,
To constantly absorb and
   constantly radiate,
To reduce earth, sea and sky
   and all that in them is
   to a single being so wholly
   that nothing whatever is withheld,
To be prepared at any moment
   for sacrifice,
To double your personality
   in bestowing it—
      that is love.

—Theophile Gautier

I do not want to make reasons
for you
to stay,
Only reasons
for you
to return.

—jonivan

I find in you a solace . . .
like that of a warm fire reflected in
   a child's eyes.
I read in you a promise . . .
like that of a rainbow after a heartache.
I sense in you a passion . . .
like that of a penetrating kiss
   that only the heart can feel.
I see in you a destination . . .
   that only we can reach.

I feel from you a love . . .
incomparable and ever-new.
I recognize in you . . .
the warmth the sunrise offers
and the peace it bestows.
In you I find all that is meaningful. . .
The dew on the morning grass,
the rain on my shoulders,
and the everlasting sun
in my heart.

—Janice Lamb

Every day I live
I discover
more and more
how impossible it is
for me
to live without you.

—James Hackman

I see the way you smile,
   the way you reach out to me
I see the way you listen
   when I need to talk
The way you make me feel special
   when I am feeling down
The way you make me happy
   when I feel like crying
The way I feel close to you
   even though we are apart
The way I feel your love
   across many miles
And seeing these things . . .
   I know we are never apart.

—Donna Wayland

With you
I would like to spend a
snowbound afternoon by a fire

I would like to walk on the
shore of a lake on a summer night

I would like to fly the sky
in a many-colored balloon

I would like to find some quiet
place for just a few moments today

I would like to feel the comfort
of my head on your shoulder

With you
   I would like to stay

—Jennifer Sue Oatey

each day and night
　　i feel your presence
you may not be near to touch
but you are in my mind and heart
you meet my needs so silently
i am not alone because of you

—diane westlake

Having you in my life . . .
I feel as though
I've been given another chance
    to live and to love.
There is a very different world
    going on inside of me now;
a world that knows peace,
    content
     self-confidence
      self-pride
       and happiness.
A world where love goes on forever.
Thank you for being a part of my new world.

—Larry Maras

I like the me I am
   when I'm with you
I like to think it's who
   I really am . . .
Growing and becoming
   more of me
In the sunlight of your love

I can't be with you
   all the time,
But what I gain in those
   hours together
Shapes the larger,
   warmer person
Who meets the rest of my world.

—Sherry Castello

If I had
a single flower
for everytime I think about you,
I could walk forever
    in my garden.

—Claudia Adrienne Grandi

Wherever I am,
you are there
also.

—Ludwig van Beethoven

I am in the world
to love you . . .
to love you and to want you.
To need you, to feel you, to touch you,
   to be with you.
I love you in the morning,
the middle of the day,
in the hours we are together,
and the hours you are away.
I love the old and the new,
the sunlight and the shade,
the warmth and the cool,
the smiles and the tears . . .

for it is only because I love you
that any of these things exist.
I love you because I was searching
for the true meanings of love
that I did not know until
I found them in you.
Those things I have learned
through and because of you.

You are all I love.
You are my love.

—jonivan

Our love
will survive the space
between us

No distance
can alter
our feelings
for each other

for we're truly
in love.

—Holly Sobey

You don't have to
call me often,
but I like
you to call.
You don't have to
tell me you love me,
but I like it when you do...
I am aware
of your feelings,
near or far,
spoken or not.

—Rosalyn Brown

Love is . . .

the most special word in our
    whisperings together—
for the stronger it becomes,
the softer it is spoken

Love is . . .

a daily adventure, a lasting goal
sharing the routines of life—
    home, work, basic matters
along with the sharing of a treasured
commitment
    to make the most of each day
    and the least of life's problems

Love is . . .

a beautiful balance
between real and imaginary worlds . . .

finding that your feet are planted
firmly on the ground
while your head is in the clouds . . .

Love is . . .

giving and taking
the best life has to offer . . .
giving without reserve
    a gift never ending
taking, accepting freely
    a gift ever-opening

Such is the love
    I'd love
    to share with you.

—Jamie Delere

For all you have done
  for the gifts you have given
For the love you have shown
  in the life we are living . . .
  I thank you
  with the whole of
    my heart.

—Andrew Tawney

It happens so seldom that we meet someone really special, that when such a person does happen along, it's a feeling of being a child again and experiencing the butterflies, the nervousness, and the blushing insecurity of caring and hoping to be cared for in return.

—James Bruce Joseph Sievers

Let us always
tell each other
our slightest griefs,
our smallest joys . . .
These confidences,
this exquisite intimacy,
are both the right
and the duty of love.

—Victor Hugo

Words are so
inadequate to
express the overwhelming
sense of feelings
I have
for you
I feel excited
and elated
I feel strong
and confident
I feel stable
and warm
Though I can't really
explain how
I feel
I do know that
I am very happy
inside
Thank you

—Susan Polis Schutz

You have always been there when I needed you. Even though we don't always agree with each other, our love has always prevailed. You have taught me kindness and understanding—you have given me the ability to find love in the world.

—Andrew Harding Allen

Together we have found
peace within ourselves,
happiness, joy, excitement,
faith and hope.
And together we have found
something much more beautiful
than words could ever express.

For together we have found . . .
love.

—Karen Meditz

We have something special
that no one
   no distance
   no time
   can take away . . .
we have each other.

—Andrew Tawney

Thank you
　　for the times alone
　　and the quietness of your touch
for the times we've talked
　　and the honesty of your thoughts
for the times in the afternoon
　　when we watch the world together
for the times in the night
　　when I don't have to dream.

Thank you
　　for letting me
　　　　love you.

—Jennifer Sue Oatey

In order to have
    a successful relationship
you need to put out of your mind
any lessons learned
    from previous relationships
because if you carry
    a sensitivity or fear with you
you won't be acting freely
and you won't let yourself
    be really known

In order to have
    a successful relationship
it is essential that both people
be completely open and honest

—Susan Polis Schutz

ACKNOWLEDGMENTS

We gratefully acknowledge the permission granted by the following authors, publishers and authors' representatives to reprint poems and excerpts from their publications.

Daniel Haughian for "Even if a day." Copyright © Daniel Haughian, 1981. All rights reserved. Reprinted by permission.

Donna Pawluk for "I promise you my love." Copyright © Donna Pawluk, 1981. All rights reserved. Reprinted by permission.

Velvet Apple Music for "I want to love you," by Dolly Parton. From the song WITH YOU by Dolly Parton. © Copyright 1972 by Owepar Publishing Co. All rights reserved. Reprinted by permission.

Linda DuPuy Moore for "Thank you." Copyright © Linda DuPuy Moore, 1980. And for "When I was young." Copyright © Linda DuPuy Moore, 1981. All rights reserved. Reprinted by permission.

Kathy Ward for "Is it possible." Copyright © Kathy Ward, 1980. All rights reserved. Reprinted by permission.

Dale F. Mead for "I fell in love." Copyright © Dale F. Mead, 1980. All rights reserved. Reprinted by permission.

Ken Lewis for "When you want." Copyright © Ken Lewis, 1980. All rights reserved. Reprinted by permission.

Jenny Deeter for "Because of your love." Copyright © Jenny Deeter, 1980. All rights reserved. Reprinted by permission.

Roger C. Van Horn for "I cannot promise you." Copyright © Roger C. Van Horn, 1980. All rights reserved. Reprinted by permission.

Sue Mitchell for "Our love is strengthened." Copyright © Sue Mitchell, 1980. All rights reserved. Reprinted by permission.

Janice Lamb for "I find in you." Copyright © Janice Lamb, 1980. All rights reserved. Reprinted by permission.

Donna Wayland for "I see the way you smile." Copyright © Donna Wayland, 1980. All rights reserved. Reprinted by permission.

Jennifer Sue Oatey for "With you" and "Thank you." Copyright © Jennifer Sue Oatey, 1981. All rights reserved. Reprinted by permission.

Diane Westlake for "each day and night." Copyright © Diane Westlake, 1977. All rights reserved. Reprinted by permission.

Larry Maras for "Having you in my life . . ." Copyright © Larry Maras, 1980. All rights reserved. Reprinted by permission.

Sherry Castello for "I like the me I am." Copyright © Sherry Boyd Castello, 1980. All rights reserved. Reprinted by permission.

Claudia Adrienne Grandi for "If I had." Copyright © Claudia Adrienne Grandi, 1974. All rights reserved. Reprinted by permission.

Holly Sobey for "Our love." Copyright © Holly Sobey, 1980. All rights reserved. Reprinted by permission.

Rosalyn Brown for "You don't have to call." Copyright © Rosalyn Brown, 1980. All rights reserved. Reprinted by permission.

jonivan for "I do not want to make reasons." From THE THOUGHT WELL. Copyright © jonivan, 1975. And for "I am in the world." Copyright © jonivan, 1980. All rights reserved. Reprinted by permission.

Starboard Publishing Company for "It happens so seldom," by James Bruce Joseph Sievers. Copyright © Starboard Publishing Company, 1976. All rights reserved. Reprinted by permission.

Karen Meditz for "Together we have found." Copyright © Karen Meditz, 1980. All rights reserved. Reprinted by permission.

If any error or omission has occurred, it is completely inadvertent, and we would like to correct it in future editions provided that written notification is made to the publisher: Blue Mountain Press, Inc., P.O. Box 4549, Boulder, Colorado 80306